D0629204

I Can Read
It Myself

Museum Reading Book
for the Very Young

FEATURING PAINTINGS
FROM THE STATE
HERMITAGE MUSEUM

SAINT PETERSBURG
2012

arca publishers

MUSEUM

Saint Petersburg

river

embankment

palace

The Hermitage

The Winter Palace seen from the Neva embankment

MUSEUM

gallery

walls

ceiling

skylight

pictures

MUSEUM

sculpture

figure

statue

marble

pedestal

PORTRAIT

face

eyes

nose

lips

ear

PORTRAIT

Anthony Van Dyck
Portrait of Elizabeth and Philadelphia Wharton, 1635–40

sisters

curls

necklace

dress

buttons

PORTRAIT

boy

smile

hands

basket

dog

Bartholome Esteban Murillo
Boy with a Dog, 1655–60

PORTRAIT

girl

parrot

feather

beak

tree

Christina Robertson
Children with a Parrot, 1850s

LANDSCAPE

hill

shepherd

field

sheep

cow

LANDSCAPE

boat

sail

water

sky

clouds

LANDSCAPE

winter

ice

people

horse

sleigh

Abraham Beerstraten
Winter View of Leyden, 1660

STILL LIFE

fruit

grapes

leaves

peaches

nut

STILL LIFE

jug

bottle

glass

knife

table

STILL LIFE

bouquet

flowers

buds

vase

cherries

Georg Flegel
Still Life with Flowers and Food, 1630–33

Can you find the picture?

Please help your child to find the pictures from which the details on the opposite page come